EASY E COOKBOOK

THE EFFORTLESS CHEF SERIES

By
Chef Maggie Chow
Copyright © 2015 by Saxonberg Associates
All rights reserved

Published by
BookSumo, a division of Saxonberg Associates
http://www.booksumo.com/

Stay To the End of the Cookbook and Receive....

I really appreciate when people, take the time to read all of my recipes.

So, as a gift for reading this entire cookbook you will receive a **massive collection of special recipes.**

Read to the end of this cookbook and get my ***Easy Specialty Cookbook Box Set for FREE***!

This box set includes the following:

1. ***Easy Sushi Cookbook***
2. ***Easy Dump Dinner Cookbook***
3. ***Easy Beans Cookbook***

Remember this box set is about **EASY** cooking.

In the ***Easy Sushi Cookbook*** you will learn the easiest methods to prepare almost every type of Japanese Sushi i.e. *California Rolls, the Perfect Sushi Rice, Crab Rolls, Osaka Style Sushi*, and so many others.

Then we go on to *Dump Dinners.* Nothing can be easier than a Dump Dinner. In the ***Easy Dump Dinner Cookbook*** we will learn how to master our slow cookers and make some amazingly unique dinners that will take almost *no effort*.

Finally in the ***Easy Beans Cookbook*** we tackle one of my favorite side dishes: Beans. There are so many delicious ways to make Baked Beans and Bean Salads that I had to share them.

So stay till the end and then keep on cooking with my *Easy Specialty Cookbook Box Set*!

About the Author.

Maggie Chow is the author and creator of your favorite *Easy Cookbooks* and *The Effortless Chef Series*. Maggie is a lover of all things related to food. Maggie loves nothing more than finding new recipes, trying them out, and then making them her own, by adding or removing ingredients, tweaking cooking times, and anything to make the recipe not only taste better, but be easier to cook!

For a complete listing of all my books please see my author page.

INTRODUCTION

Welcome to *The Effortless Chef Series*! Thank you for taking the time to download the *Easy Broccoli Cookbook*. Come take a journey with me into the delights of easy cooking. The point of this cookbook and all my cookbooks is to exemplify the effortless nature of cooking simply.

In this book we focus on Broccoli. You will find that even though the recipes are simple, the taste of the dishes is quite amazing.

So will you join me in an adventure of simple cooking? If the answer is yes (and I hope it is) please consult the table of contents to find the dishes you are most interested in. Once you are ready jump right in and start cooking.

— Chef Maggie Chow

TABLE OF CONTENTS

Contents

STAY TO THE END OF THE COOKBOOK AND RECEIVE.. 2

About the Author. 5

Introduction 7

Table of Contents 8

Any Issues? Contact Me 13

Legal Notes 14

Common Abbreviations 15

Chapter 1: All About Broccoli 16

   The Different Types of Broccoli....... 16

   Shopping for Broccoli. The Right Way. 17

   Broccoli and Its Proper Storage 18

   Methods of Cooking Broccoli for Optimal Nutritional Value 19

Dealing with the Bitterness of Broccoli and Awaking its Natural Sweetness 21

Chapter 2: Easy Broccoli Recipes 23

Artisan Broccoli Soup I 23

Asian Style Broccoli with Beef I 26

Soup of Broccoli, Potatoes, Onions, and Cheese 29

Broccoli Bake I 32

(Red Onions and Sage) 32

Garlic Broccoli and Cashews 35

Broccoli Salad I 38

(Bacon, Raisins, and Sunflowers) ... 38

Lemon Broccoli Steamer 41

Broccoli Bake II 44

(Broccoli, Creamy Mushrooms, and Cheddar) 44

Artisan Broccoli Soup II 47

Italian Style Broccoli and Pasta 50

Easy Creamy Broccoli and Chicken 53

Quiche I 56

(Broccoli, Onions, and Mozzarella) . 56

Broccoli Salad II 59

(Bacon, Cheddar, and Broccoli) 59

Broccoli Salad III 62

(Bacon, Raisins, Pasta) 62

Restaurant Style Broccoli and Pasta 65

Asian Style Broccoli and Chicken ... 69

Broccoli Salad IV.............................. 72

(Peanuts and Ramen)...................... 72

Honey Mustard Chicken and Broccoli 75

Asian Style Broccoli and Beef II 78

Broccoli Salad V............................... 81

(Bacon, Tomatoes, and Tortellini) ... 81

Artisan Broccoli Soup III................... 84

Broccoli Bake III 87

(French Fries, Mushroom Soup, and Ham).. 87

Broccoli Bake IV............................... 90

(Brown Rice, Walnuts, and Cheddar) 90

Broccoli Tots 93
Easy Broccoli and Quinoa 96
Broccoli Cheese Soup III 102
Sweet and Creamy Broccoli 105
Broccoli in Venice 108
Cream of Everything Casserole 111
Seattle Style Broccoli Soup 114
Green and White Broccoli 117
Maggie's Easy Beef and Broccoli .. 120
Creamy Broccoli 123
American Casserole 126
Cream of Mushrooms and Broccoli 129
Countryside Broccoli Soup 132
Southeast Asian Broccoli 135
Alfredo Broccoli 138
Artisan Style Broccoli Soup II 141
Sour Cream Condensed Broccoli .. 144
Asian Style Broccoli and Beef 147
Red Pepper Broccoli 150
Crackers and Broccoli Bake 152
Basil Broccoli 155

A Quiche of Broccoli 158

Maggie's Easy Broccoli Stir Fry 161

2 Cheese Chicken Casserole........ 164

Restaurant Style Broccoli.............. 168

Parmesan Rabe 170

Swiss Style Broccoli Casserole..... 172

THANKS FOR READING! NOW LET'S TRY SOME **SUSHI** AND **DUMP DINNERS**...... 175

Come On… 177

Let's Be Friends :) 177

Can I Ask A Favour? 178

Interested in Other Easy Cookbooks?
.... 179

Any Issues? Contact Me

If you find that something important to you is missing from this book please contact me at maggie@booksumo.com.

I will try my best to re-publish a revised copy taking your feedback into consideration and let you know when the book has been revised with you in mind.

:)

— Chef Maggie Chow

LEGAL NOTES

ALL RIGHTS RESERVED. NO PART OF THIS BOOK MAY BE REPRODUCED OR TRANSMITTED IN ANY FORM OR BY ANY MEANS. PHOTOCOPYING, POSTING ONLINE, AND / OR DIGITAL COPYING IS STRICTLY PROHIBITED UNLESS WRITTEN PERMISSION IS GRANTED BY THE BOOK'S PUBLISHING COMPANY. LIMITED USE OF THE BOOK'S TEXT IS PERMITTED FOR USE IN REVIEWS WRITTEN FOR THE PUBLIC AND/OR PUBLIC DOMAIN.

COMMON ABBREVIATIONS

cup(s)	C.
tablespoon	tbsp
teaspoon	tsp
ounce	oz.
pound	lb

*All units used are standard American measurements

Chapter 1: All About Broccoli

The Different Types of Broccoli

There are three main types of broccoli that you will encounter when taking a trip to the grocery store.

1. Broccoli rabe
2. Broccolini
3. Broccoli Romanesco
4. Regular Broccoli

Broccoli rabe is the closest relative to normal broccoli. Except that it is a quite bitter. You will usually find this type of broccoli cooked in European style dishes.

Broccolini is a hybrid vegetable. A crossbreed between regular broccoli and Chinese kale.

Broccoli Romanesco is a lighter green version of normal broccoli.

The Romanesco type of broccoli is a perfect mathematical vegetable.

The florets of this type of broccoli are natural occurrences of mathematical fractals.

Meaning these florets are a perfectly infinite repeating pattern.

And finally you have the regular broccoli we all know and love.

This is the type of broccoli we focus mainly on this cookbook.

SHOPPING FOR BROCCOLI. THE RIGHT WAY.

Finding a healthy head of broccoli in the grocery store is not too hard.

Your broccoli florets should be grouped together tightly and the stalks should be tightly bunched together as well.

The overall color of the broccoli should be bright green and the stems should not be moist.

Find a tightly bunched head of broccoli that is bright green and you are all set!

BROCCOLI AND ITS PROPER STORAGE

Most modern day fridges have two cabinets at the bottom. These cabinets are made particularly for the storage of fruits and vegetables.

You want to store your broccoli in one of these compartments.

But place the broccoli in a resealable plastic bag first. Perforate the plastic bag with some holes.

To do this simply by taking a knife or a fork and poking some holes into the bag. Maybe 5 to 10 holes distributed evenly throughout the bag will do.

Place your bag of broccoli in the lower cabinet if your fridge and that is it.

The broccoli should stay fresh for multiple days using this manner of storage.

METHODS OF COOKING BROCCOLI FOR OPTIMAL NUTRITIONAL VALUE

There are essentially three ways to cook broccoli: steaming, boiling, and roasting.

Overall when cooking broccoli you should try to use a high heat and cook it quickly for the best results.

The least preferably way to cook your broccoli is to boil it constantly. Although this is the easiest method and one we will make use of in this cookbook.

The problem with boiling broccoli is: it is very easy to overcook it.

It's very important to following the timing instructions closely in this cookbook when boiling to avoid overcooking.

Boiling broccoli causes a lot of the nutrients in the florets to escape into the surrounding water.

To harvest the most nutrients from broccoli. One of the best ways to prepare it, is with steam.

The problem with steaming broccoli is the florets will always cook faster than the stems.

Therefore, if you are cooking only the florets. Use a steamer insert or a steamer basket, and steam the florets over boiling water for about 6 mins.

To cook both the florets and the stems at the same time. Use the following hybrid steaming and boiling method.

Take your broccoli and separate the florets from the stalks.

Place only the stalks in a pan.

Add just enough water to submerge the stalks. Then place the florets directly over the stalks.

The florets should be sitting above the water and the stalks should be completely submerged.

Now place a lid on the pan and let everything cook for 4 mins, with a high level of heat, then turn the heat down to low, and cook the broccoli for 4 more mins, again with the lid placed on the pot.

DEALING WITH THE BITTERNESS OF BROCCOLI AND AWAKING ITS NATURAL SWEETNESS

If you want to avoid the bitterness in broccoli. The best way to do this is to cook with only dry heat.

Therefore baking the broccoli in the oven will be the best option.

The dry heat of the oven will heighten the natural sugars in the vegetable and result in a less bitter taste.

The best way to experience a less bitter broccoli is to cook a rustic style broccoli roast.

To do this cut your broccoli and its stems into bite size pieces.

Coat everything with some olive oil and sprinkle the veggies with some garlic power and black pepper.

Toss everything with some tongs then add in your preferred amount of salt.

Place the veggies in a casserole dish and put it all in the oven at 425 degrees for 10 to 12 minutes.

This rustic style broccoli roast is the sweetest version of the vegetable you can cook without adding extra sugars.

Before serving your rustic broccoli roast top it with some parmesan and taste the difference!

Chapter 2: Easy Broccoli Recipes

Artisan Broccoli Soup I

Ingredients

- 8 C. chicken broth
- 1 (10.75 oz.) can condensed cream of mushroom soup
- 3/4 C. chopped onion
- 3/4 C. chopped celery
- 1 tbsp salt
- 1 pinch ground white pepper
- 2 C. milk
- 1/3 C. cornstarch
- 1/4 C. water
- 3 C. fresh broccoli florets, cooked
- 1 1/2 C. shredded American cheese
- 1 1/2 C. shredded Cheddar cheese

Directions

- Get a bowl, combine until smooth: water and cornstarch. Set it aside.
- Boil the following in a big pot: pepper, broth, salt, mushroom soup, celery, and onions. Once boiling, place a lid on the pot and lower the heat. Let the soup lightly boil for 22 mins.
- Pour in your milk and then get the soup boiling once more. Slowly add in your cornstarch mix while stirring. Let the contents lightly boil for 7 mins.
- Now finally add in your cheese and broccoli. Once the cheese is fully melted. Shut the heat.
- Enjoy.

Amount per serving (8 total)

Timing Information:

Preparation	Cooking	Total Time
10 m	40 m	1 h

Nutritional Information:

Calories	309 kcal
Fat	18.8 g
Carbohydrates	16g
Protein	18.5 g
Cholesterol	50 mg
Sodium	2389 mg

* Percent Daily Values are based on a 2,000 calorie diet.

Asian Style Broccoli with Beef I

Ingredients

- 1/4 C. all-purpose flour
- 1 (10.5 oz.) can beef broth
- 2 tbsps white sugar
- 2 tbsps soy sauce
- 1 lb boneless round steak, cut into bite size pieces
- 1/4 tsp chopped fresh ginger root
- 1 clove garlic, minced
- 4 C. chopped fresh broccoli

Directions

- Get a bowl, combine until smooth: soy sauce, flour, sugar, and broth.
- Now stir fry your beef for 5 mins and add the soy sauce mix, broccoli, garlic, and ginger. Get

the contents simmering with a high heat and then lower it.
- Let the soy sauce mix get thick while lightly boiling for about 7 to 12 mins.
- Enjoy with jasmine rice.

Amount per serving (4 total)

Timing Information:

Preparation	Cooking	Total Time
15 m	15 m	30 m

Nutritional Information:

Calories	178 kcal
Fat	3.2 g
Carbohydrates	19g
Protein	19.2 g
Cholesterol	39 mg
Sodium	755 mg

* Percent Daily Values are based on a 2,000 calorie diet.

Soup of Broccoli, Potatoes, Onions, and Cheese

Ingredients

- 1 onion, diced
- 1 tbsp olive oil
- 2 heads broccoli, chopped
- 2 potatoes, peeled and cubed
- 4 C. chicken broth
- 4 oz. stilton cheese

Directions

- Stir fry your onions in olive oil until see-through. Then add in your potatoes and broccoli and cook for 6 mins. Then add the broth and get the contents boiling. Once the broth is boiling set the heat to a lower level and let everything lightly boil for 23 mins with no cover.

- Add the cheese after shutting the heat and let it melt. Use an immersion blender or regular food processor to blend the soup down to become smoother.
- Then reheat it before serving.
- Enjoy.

Amount per serving (6 total)

Timing Information:

Preparation	Cooking	Total Time
15 m	40 m	1 h

Nutritional Information:

Calories	183 kcal
Fat	8.1 g
Carbohydrates	21.7g
Protein	8.2 g
Cholesterol	14 mg
Sodium	297 mg

* Percent Daily Values are based on a 2,000 calorie diet.

Broccoli Bake I

(Red Onions and Sage)

Ingredients

- 1 (12 oz.) bag broccoli florets
- 1/2 red onion, sliced
- 8 fresh sage leaves, torn
- 2 tbsps extra-virgin olive oil
- 1/2 tsp salt
- 1/2 tsp garlic salt
- 1/4 tsp ground black pepper

Directions

- Cover a casserole dish or sheet for baking with foil and then set your oven to 400 degrees before doing anything else.
- Layer your broccoli evenly throughout the dish and top with sage leaves and onions. Garnish all the veggies with olive oil and

then black pepper, regular salt, and garlic salt.
- Cook the veggies in the oven for 27 mins until slightly browned and crunchy.
- Enjoy.

Amount per serving (4 total)

Timing Information:

Preparation	Cooking	Total Time
10 m	20 m	30 m

Nutritional Information:

Calories	97 kcal
Fat	7.1 g
Carbohydrates	7.3g
Protein	2.6 g
Cholesterol	0 mg
Sodium	546 mg

* Percent Daily Values are based on a 2,000 calorie diet.

Garlic Broccoli and Cashews

Ingredients

- 1 1/2 lbs fresh broccoli, cut into bite size pieces
- 1/3 C. butter
- 1 tbsp brown sugar
- 3 tbsps soy sauce
- 2 tsps white vinegar
- 1/4 tsp ground black pepper
- 2 cloves garlic, minced
- 1/3 C. chopped salted cashews

Directions

- Boil your broccoli in one inch of water for 8 mins. The remove all the liquid and place the broccoli on a plate.
- Simultaneously as you are boiling the broccoli boil the following: garlic, butter, pepper, soy sauce,

and vinegar. Once it is boiling shut the heat and add in the cashews.
- Garnish your broccoli with the soy sauce mix and serve warm.
- Enjoy.

Amount per serving (6 total)

Timing Information:

Preparation	Cooking	Total Time
10 m	10 m	20 m

Nutritional Information:

Calories	187 kcal
Fat	14.2 g
Carbohydrates	13.2g
Protein	5.1 g
Cholesterol	27 mg
Sodium	611 mg

* Percent Daily Values are based on a 2,000 calorie diet.

Broccoli Salad I

(Bacon, Raisins, and Sunflowers)

Ingredients

- 10 slices bacon
- 1 head fresh broccoli, cut into bite size pieces
- 1/4 C. red onion, chopped
- 1/2 C. raisins
- 3 tbsps white wine vinegar
- 2 tbsps white sugar
- 1 C. mayonnaise
- 1 C. sunflower seeds

Directions

- Fry your bacon. Remove any oil excesses and then break the bacon into pieces.
- Get a bowl, mix: raisins, onions, and broccoli.

- Get a 2nd bowl, combine: mayo, vinegar, and sugar.
- Combine both bowls and stir the salad to evenly coat all the florets with dressing.
- Finally add in your seeds and bacon.
- Enjoy chilled.

Amount per serving (6 total)

Timing Information:

Preparation	Cooking	Total Time
15 m	15 m	30 m

Nutritional Information:

Calories	559 kcal
Fat	48.1 g
Carbohydrates	23.9g
Protein	12.9 g
Cholesterol	31 mg
Sodium	584 mg

* Percent Daily Values are based on a 2,000 calorie diet.

Lemon Broccoli Steamer

Ingredients

- 1 lb broccoli, separated into florets
- 2 tsps fresh lemon juice
- 2 tbsps water
- 3 tbsps butter
- 2 cloves garlic, minced
- 1 pinch salt
- 2 tsps lemon juice
- 1 tsp ground black pepper

Directions

- Steam your broccoli for 16 mins in a frying pan with a lid on it in water with lemon juice (2 tsps).
- Simultaneously stir fry your garlic with salt for 9 mins in butter.
- Remove all the liquid from your broccoli and place it back in the pan, add the remaining lemon

juice, and garlic mix. Garnish the florets with pepper.
- Enjoy.

Amount per serving (4 total)

Timing Information:

Preparation	Cooking	Total Time
10 m	10 m	20 m

Nutritional Information:

Calories	120 kcal
Fat	9.1 g
Carbohydrates	8.8g
Protein	3.5 g
Cholesterol	23 mg
Sodium	100 mg

* Percent Daily Values are based on a 2,000 calorie diet.

Broccoli Bake II

(Broccoli, Creamy Mushrooms, and Cheddar)

Ingredients

- 1 (10.75 oz.) can condensed cream of mushroom soup
- 1 C. mayonnaise
- 1 egg, beaten
- 1/4 C. finely chopped onion
- 3 (10 oz.) packages frozen chopped broccoli
- 8 oz. shredded sharp Cheddar cheese
- salt to taste
- ground black pepper to taste
- 2 pinches paprika

Directions

- Coat a casserole dish with butter or oil and then set your oven to

350 degrees before doing anything else.
- Get a bowl, mix: onions, soup, eggs, and mayo. Combine in your broccoli with the mix and stir to coat the florets.
- Add your cheese and layer the contents evenly throughout your casserole dish. Top with salt, paprika, and pepper.
- Cook in the oven for 50 mins.
- Enjoy after letting the casserole sit for 10 mins.

Amount per serving (8 total)

Timing Information:

Preparation	Cooking	Total Time
15 m	1 h	1 h 15 m

Nutritional Information:

Calories	387 kcal
Fat	34.1 g
Carbohydrates	9.5g
Protein	11.3 g
Cholesterol	63 mg
Sodium	619 mg

* Percent Daily Values are based on a 2,000 calorie diet.

Artisan Broccoli Soup II

Ingredients

- 1/2 C. butter
- 1 onion, chopped
- 1 (16 oz.) package frozen chopped broccoli
- 4 (14.5 oz.) cans chicken broth
- 1 (1 lb) loaf processed cheese food, cubed
- 2 C. milk
- 1 tbsp garlic powder
- 2/3 C. cornstarch
- 1 C. water

Directions

- Get a bowl, mix until smooth: water and cornstarch.
- Stir fry your onions in butter in a big pot and then add in your broccoli and broth. Let the broth and broccoli lightly boil for 16

mins. Then set the heat to low and pour in your cheese. Once the cheese has melted season everything with the garlic powder and pour in the milk.
- Slowly stir and pour in your cornstarch mix. Let the soup cook for a bit more time (3 more mins).
- Enjoy.

Amount per serving (12 total)

Timing Information:

Preparation	Cooking	Total Time
10 m	30 m	40 m

Nutritional Information:

Calories	265 kcal
Fat	18.2 g
Carbohydrates	15.1g
Protein	10 g
Cholesterol	56 mg
Sodium	1136 mg

* Percent Daily Values are based on a 2,000 calorie diet.

Italian Style Broccoli and Pasta

Ingredients

- 1 lb spicy Italian sausage
- 1/2 C. olive oil
- 4 cloves garlic, minced
- 1 (16 oz.) package cavatelli pasta
- 1 (16 oz.) package frozen broccoli
- 1/2 tsp crushed red pepper flakes
- 1/4 C. grated Parmesan cheese

Directions

- Boil your pasta in salt and water for 10 mins. At the 7 min mark add in your broccoli to the boiling pasta. Then remove all the liquid after 10 mins of total boiling time.
- Simultaneously stir fry your sausage and set it aside after removing all the drippings.

- Add in the olive oil and the garlic and cook until golden in color.
- Get a big bowl, toss: broccoli, sausage, cavatelli, garlic, and olive oil.
- Top the mix with parmesan and pepper flakes.
- Enjoy.

Amount per serving (8 total)

Timing Information:

Preparation	Cooking	Total Time
5 m	30 m	35 m

Nutritional Information:

Calories	548 kcal
Fat	33 g
Carbohydrates	45.5g
Protein	18.4 g
Cholesterol	45 mg
Sodium	470 mg

* Percent Daily Values are based on a 2,000 calorie diet.

Easy Creamy Broccoli and Chicken

Ingredients

- 1 lb chopped fresh broccoli
- 1 1/2 C. cubed, cooked chicken meat
- 1 (10.75 oz.) can condensed cream of broccoli soup
- 1/3 C. milk
- 1/2 C. shredded Cheddar cheese
- 1 tbsp butter, melted
- 2 tbsps dried bread crumbs

Directions

- Set your oven to 450 degrees before doing anything else.
- Boil your broccoli for 6 mins in water then remove all the liquid.
- Get a bowl, combine: milk and soup.

- Put the broccoli in a pie dish and the cheese and chicken.
- Combine the crumbled bread and melted butter and then add this as well to the dish.
- Cook everything in the oven for 17 mins.
- Enjoy warm.

Amount per serving (6 total)

Timing Information:

Preparation	Cooking	Total Time
20 m	20 m	40 m

Nutritional Information:

Calories	186 kcal
Fat	8.5 g
Carbohydrates	12.2g
Protein	15.5 g
Cholesterol	44 mg
Sodium	440 mg

* Percent Daily Values are based on a 2,000 calorie diet.

Quiche I

(Broccoli, Onions, and Mozzarella)

Ingredients

- 2 tbsps butter
- 1 onion, minced
- 1 tsp minced garlic
- 2 C. chopped fresh broccoli
- 1 (9 inch) unbaked pie crust
- 1 1/2 C. shredded mozzarella cheese
- 4 eggs, well beaten
- 1 1/2 C. milk
- 1 tsp salt
- 1/2 tsp black pepper
- 1 tbsp butter, melted

Directions

- Set your oven to 350 degrees before doing anything else.

- Get a bowl, mix: milk and eggs.
- Stir fry your broccoli, onions, and garlic in melted butter until everything is tender.
- Add the veggies into the pie and top with cheese.
- Add the milk mixture, melted butter, pepper and salt.
- Cook the quiche in the oven for 40 mins.
- Enjoy.

Amount per serving (6 total)

Timing Information:

Preparation	Cooking	Total Time
20 m	30 m	50 m

Nutritional Information:

Calories	371 kcal
Fat	24.9 g
Carbohydrates	21.5g
Protein	16.1 g
Cholesterol	162 mg
Sodium	885 mg

* Percent Daily Values are based on a 2,000 calorie diet.

Broccoli Salad II

(Bacon, Cheddar, and Broccoli)

Ingredients

- 8 slices bacon
- 2 heads fresh broccoli, chopped
- 1 1/2 C. sharp Cheddar cheese, shredded
- 1/2 large red onion, chopped
- 1/4 C. red wine vinegar
- 1/8 C. white sugar
- 2 tsps ground black pepper
- 1 tsp salt
- 2/3 C. mayonnaise
- 1 tsp fresh lemon juice

Directions

- Fry your bacon and then remove the oil and break it into pieces.

- Get a bowl, mix: onions, broccoli, bacon, and cheese.
- Get a 2nd bowl, mix: lemon juice, vinegar, mayo, sugar, salt, and pepper.
- Combine both bowls and toss to evenly coat the florets.
- Place the contents in the fridge for 20 mins.
- Enjoy chilled.

Amount per serving (12 total)

Timing Information:

Preparation	Cooking	Total Time
15 m	15 m	30 m

Nutritional Information:

Calories	273 kcal
Fat	24 g
Carbohydrates	7.3g
Protein	8.1 g
Cholesterol	35 mg
Sodium	543 mg

* Percent Daily Values are based on a 2,000 calorie diet.

Broccoli Salad III

(Bacon, Raisins, Pasta)

Ingredients

- 6 slices bacon
- 20 oz. fresh cheese-filled tortellini
- 1/2 C. mayonnaise
- 1/2 C. white sugar
- 2 tsps cider vinegar
- 3 heads fresh broccoli, cut into florets
- 1 C. raisins
- 1 C. sunflower seeds
- 1 red onion, finely chopped

Directions

- Get a bowl, mix: vinegar, sugar, and mayo.
- Fry your bacon and remove excess oils and then break the bacon into pieces.

- Boil your pasta in salt and water for 9 mins. Then remove all the liquid from the pot.
- In a 2nd big bowl, combine: pasta, red onions, Broccoli, seeds, raisins, and bacon.
- Toss everything in the mayo mix.
- Enjoy chilled.

Amount per serving (12 total)

Timing Information:

Preparation	Cooking	Total Time
10 m	20 m	30 m

Nutritional Information:

Calories	322 kcal
Fat	16.1 g
Carbohydrates	38.7g
Protein	9 g
Cholesterol	20 mg
Sodium	341 mg

* Percent Daily Values are based on a 2,000 calorie diet.

Restaurant Style Broccoli and Pasta

Ingredients

- 1 (12 oz.) package angel hair pasta
- 2 1/2 tbsps butter, divided
- 1 1/2 tbsps all-purpose flour
- 1 1/2 C. milk
- 1/2 C. heavy cream
- 1 1/2 tbsps pesto
- 1 1/2 tbsps chopped fresh parsley
- 3 cloves garlic, minced
- 2 tbsps grated Parmesan cheese
- 2 tsps salt, divided
- 1/2 tsp ground white pepper
- 1 dash Worcestershire sauce
- 1 dash hot sauce
- 1/2 (16 oz.) package frozen broccoli florets, thawed
- 1 lb jumbo shrimp, peeled and deveined

- 3 cloves garlic, minced

Directions

- Steam your broccoli in 2 inches of water with a steamer insert for 7 mins.
- Now begin boiling your pasta in salt and water for 9 mins. Then remove all the liquid.
- Make a roux simultaneously with butter (1.5 tbsps) and flour.
- Cook for about 2 mins stirring constantly make sure to not burn the flour.
- Add in the cream and milk and get the contents lightly boiling with a low level of heat and constant stirring.
- Now add in: Worcestershire, pesto, white pepper, parsley, salt (1 tsp), garlic cloves, and parmesan.
- Finally fry your shrimp in 1 tbsp of butter and then add in 3 more

cloves of garlic, and 1 tsp of salt. Stir fry the shrimp for 6 mins.
- Get a big bowl, and toss: broccoli, pasta, and shrimp with the sauce.
- Enjoy.

Amount per serving (6 total)

Timing Information:

Preparation	Cooking	Total Time
30 m	30 m	1 h

Nutritional Information:

Calories	431 kcal
Fat	19.9 g
Carbohydrates	39.5g
Protein	24.3 g
Cholesterol	145 mg
Sodium	1139 mg

* Percent Daily Values are based on a 2,000 calorie diet.

Asian Style Broccoli and Chicken

Ingredients

- 3 C. broccoli florets
- 1 tbsp olive oil
- 2 skinless, boneless chicken breast halves - cut into 1 inch strips
- 1/4 C. sliced green onions
- 4 cloves garlic, thinly sliced
- 1 tbsp hoisin sauce
- 1 tbsp chili paste
- 1 tbsp low sodium soy sauce
- 1/2 tsp ground ginger
- 1/4 tsp crushed red pepper
- 1/2 tsp salt
- 1/2 tsp black pepper
- 1/8 C. chicken stock

Directions

- With a steamer insert and 2 inches of water steam your broccoli for 6 mins.
- Now stir fry: garlic, chicken, and green onions until the chicken is fully done.
- Add in with the chicken the following: chicken stock, soy sauce, black pepper, ginger, salt, red pepper, chili paste, and hoisin.
- Get the broth boiling and let it continue boiling for 4 mins. Now add in your broccoli and let it cook until the sauce thickens for about 1 more min.
- Enjoy with jasmine rice.

Amount per serving (4 total)

Timing Information:

Preparation	Cooking	Total Time
10 m	20 m	30 m

Nutritional Information:

Calories	156 kcal
Fat	6.2 g
Carbohydrates	10.9g
Protein	15.9 g
Cholesterol	36 mg
Sodium	606 mg

* Percent Daily Values are based on a 2,000 calorie diet.

Broccoli Salad IV

(Peanuts and Ramen)

Ingredients

- 1 (16 oz.) package broccoli coleslaw mix
- 2 (3 oz.) packages chicken flavored ramen noodles
- 1 bunch green onions, chopped
- 1 C. unsalted peanuts
- 1 C. sunflower seeds
- 1/2 C. white sugar
- 1/4 C. vegetable oil
- 1/3 C. cider vinegar

Directions

- Get a bowl, mix: green onions, vinegar, sugar, crushed ramen and its seasoning, oil, and slaw.
- Toss the slaw mix and then add seeds and peanuts.

- Enjoy chilled after 20 mins in the fridge.

Amount per serving (6 total)

Timing Information:

Preparation	Cooking	Total Time
15 m		45 m

Nutritional Information:

Calories	562 kcal
Fat	34.4 g
Carbohydrates	52.3g
Protein	16.5 g
Cholesterol	0 mg
Sodium	356 mg

* Percent Daily Values are based on a 2,000 calorie diet.

Honey Mustard Chicken and Broccoli

Ingredients

- 2 C. chopped, cooked chicken meat
- 2 C. fresh chopped broccoli
- 1/2 C. chopped onion
- 2 tbsps honey
- 1/2 C. chopped green bell pepper
- 1 1/2 C. shredded Cheddar cheese
- 1/2 C. mayonnaise
- 2 tbsps Dijon-style prepared mustard
- salt and pepper to taste
- 1 tbsp minced garlic
- 1 (8 oz.) package refrigerated crescent rolls

Directions

- Set your oven to 400 degrees before doing anything else.
- Get a bowl, mix: garlic, chicken, pepper, broccoli, salt, honey, onions, mustard, bell peppers, mayo, and cheese.
- Line a baking dish or casserole dish with foil.
- Get a 2nd bowl and place it upside down on the dish and roll out your dough around the top of the bowl.
- Add some chicken to the rolled out dough and fold to form a roll around the mix.
- Repeat for any remaining dough or mixture.
- Place the roll on the sheet and cook in the oven for 27 mins.
- Enjoy.

Amount per serving (16 total)

Timing Information:

Preparation	Cooking	Total Time
10 m	30 m	40 m

Nutritional Information:

Calories	183 kcal
Fat	12.7 g
Carbohydrates	7.8g
Protein	8.9 g
Cholesterol	27 mg
Sodium	275 mg

* Percent Daily Values are based on a 2,000 calorie diet.

Asian Style Broccoli and Beef II

Ingredients

- 2 tbsps low-sodium soy sauce
- 2 tbsps fat-free Italian dressing
- 1 tsp cornstarch
- 1 tbsp minced garlic
- 1 tsp ground ginger
- 3/4 lb round steak, cut into strips
- 6 C. water
- 5 cubes beef bouillon
- 4 oz. linguine pasta, uncooked
- 1/2 C. fat free beef broth
- 1 C. fresh mushrooms, sliced
- 1/2 C. sliced green onion
- 1 lb broccoli, separated into florets

Directions

- Get a bowl, combine: ginger, soy sauce, garlic, steak, cornstarch, and dressing.
- Cover the bowl with plastic wrap and place it in the fridge for 20 mins.
- Simultaneously while the steak is soaking boil your pasta in water and bouillon for 9 mins. The remove the excess liquid.
- Stir fry your beef for 3 mins until browned and cooked through and add in the broth, onions, and mushrooms. Get the broth boiling and then place a lid on the pan and let the contents lightly boil for 7 mins.
- Take off the lid and input your broccoli and stir the mix until you find that the broccoli is a bit soft and bright in colour.
- Finally combine the beef and sauce with the pasta and stir to evenly coat.
- Enjoy.

Amount per serving (4 total)

Timing Information:

Preparation	Cooking	Total Time
15 m	45 m	1 h

Nutritional Information:

Calories	303 kcal
Fat	7.1 g
Carbohydrates	35.1g
Protein	26.4 g
Cholesterol	46 mg
Sodium	1533 mg

* Percent Daily Values are based on a 2,000 calorie diet.

Broccoli Salad V

(Bacon, Tomatoes, and Tortellini)

Ingredients

- 2 (9 oz.) packages refrigerated three-cheese tortellini
- 1 lb bacon
- 4 C. chopped broccoli
- 1 pint grape tomatoes, halved
- 2 green onions, finely chopped
- 1 C. bottled coleslaw dressing

Directions

- Boil your pasta in water and salt for about 8 mins then remove all the liquid and place the pasta in the fridge and in a bowl for 35 mins.
- Fry your bacon for 9 to 12 mins, remove excess oils and then

place the bacon on paper towels. Now break it into pieces after a good amount of grease has been absorbed by the towels.
- Get a big bowl, toss: green onions, pasta, tomatoes, dressing, broccoli, and bacon.
- Place the mix in the fridge for 10 to 20 min until fully chilled then serve.
- Enjoy.

Amount per serving (10 total)

Timing Information:

Preparation	Cooking	Total Time
15 m	15 m	1 h 30 m

Nutritional Information:

Calories	349 kcal
Fat	18.2 g
Carbohydrates	33.6g
Protein	13.9 g
Cholesterol	47 mg
Sodium	736 mg

* Percent Daily Values are based on a 2,000 calorie diet.

Artisan Broccoli Soup III

Ingredients

- 1 C. sliced carrots
- 2 C. chopped broccoli
- 1 C. water
- 1 tsp chicken bouillon granules
- 1/4 C. chopped onion
- 1/4 C. butter
- 1/4 C. all-purpose flour
- 1/4 tsp ground black pepper
- 2 C. milk
- 2 C. shredded sharp Cheddar cheese

Directions

- Get the following boiling in a large pot: bouillon, carrots, water, and broccoli.
- Once the contents are boiling place a lid on the pan and let the contents simmer over a low heat

for 7 mins. Place everything to the side.
- In another big pot fry your onions in butter until see-through and add in pepper and flour. Let this cook for 1 min while stirring. Then add in your milk. Get everything boiling and then add in your cheese once the cheese has fully melted, pour in your vegetables and liquid.
- Get the mix hot and then serve in bowls.
- Enjoy.

Amount per serving (4 total)

Timing Information:

Preparation	Cooking	Total Time
15 m	15 m	30 m

Nutritional Information:

Calories	449 kcal
Fat	33 g
Carbohydrates	18.9g
Protein	20.6 g
Cholesterol	100 mg
Sodium	523 mg

* Percent Daily Values are based on a 2,000 calorie diet.

Broccoli Bake III

(French Fries, Mushroom Soup, and Ham)

Ingredients

- 1 (16 oz.) package frozen French fries
- 1 (16 oz.) package frozen chopped broccoli
- 1 1/2 C. cooked, cubed ham
- 1 (10.75 oz.) can condensed cream of mushroom soup
- 1 (10.75 oz.) can milk
- 1/4 C. mayonnaise
- 1 C. grated Parmesan cheese

Directions

- Set your oven to 375 degrees before doing anything else.
- Get a bowl, mix: mayo, soup, and milk.

- Now get a casserole dish and layer your fries in it evenly. Then add: soup mix, broccoli, ham, and cheese.
- Cook the casserole in the oven for 43 mins.
- Enjoy.

Amount per serving (5 total)

Timing Information:

Preparation	Cooking	Total Time
5 m	40 m	45 m

Nutritional Information:

Calories	502 kcal
Fat	31.2 g
Carbohydrates	34.7g
Protein	22.8 g
Cholesterol	49 mg
Sodium	1626 mg

* Percent Daily Values are based on a 2,000 calorie diet.

Broccoli Bake IV

(Brown Rice, Walnuts, and Cheddar)

Ingredients

- 1/2 C. chopped walnuts
- 1 tbsp butter
- 1 onion, chopped
- 1/2 tsp minced garlic
- 1 C. uncooked instant brown rice
- 1 C. vegetable broth
- 1 lb fresh broccoli florets
- 1/2 tsp salt
- 1/8 tsp ground black pepper
- 1 C. shredded Cheddar cheese

Directions

- Set your oven to 350 degrees before doing anything else. Once heated, toast your walnuts in a casserole dish for 7 mins.

- Stir fry your garlic and onions in butter for 5 mins and then add the broth and rice.
- Once the contents are boiling, lower the heat and place a lid on the pan.
- Let the contents cook for 10 mins with a light simmer.
- Simultaneously microwave your broccoli after topping it with pepper and salt until soft.
- Create your individual serving plates by adding some rice and then some broccoli and walnuts with a final layer of cheese.
- Enjoy hot.

Amount per serving (4 total)

Timing Information:

Preparation	Cooking	Total Time
15 m	25 m	40 m

Nutritional Information:

Calories	368 kcal
Fat	22.9 g
Carbohydrates	30.4g
Protein	15.1 g
Cholesterol	37 mg
Sodium	643 mg

* Percent Daily Values are based on a 2,000 calorie diet.

Broccoli Tots

Ingredients

- 3 tbsps prepared Dijon-style mustard
- 4 tbsps honey
- 2 C. broccoli florets
- 1 C. shredded Cheddar cheese
- 1 egg
- 1 C. milk
- 1/2 C. sifted all-purpose flour
- 1/2 tsp baking powder
- 1/2 tsp salt
- 1/2 tsp vegetable oil
- 1/2 C. vegetable oil for frying

Directions

- Get a bowl, mix: honey and mustard.
- Get a deep fryer or large skillet and heat your oil to 375 degrees for frying later.

- Dice your broccoli and then blend them in a blender and place everything in a 2nd bowl with cheese.
- Get a 3rd bowl, beat with .5 tsp of oil: milk, salt, whisked eggs, baking powder, and flour.
- Combine the broccoli with the milk and flour mix and stir to form a thick batter.
- Fry dollops of the broccoli mix until golden.
- Once all the bite sized broccoli pieces have been fried, garnish them with the honey sauce.
- Enjoy as a unique appetizer.

Amount per serving (12 total)

Timing Information:

Preparation	Cooking	Total Time
10 m	10 m	20 m

Nutritional Information:

Calories	113 kcal
Fat	5.1 g
Carbohydrates	12.6g
Protein	4.5 g
Cholesterol	27 mg
Sodium	284 mg

* Percent Daily Values are based on a 2,000 calorie diet.

Easy Broccoli and Quinoa

Ingredients

- 2 C. chopped broccoli
- 1 3/4 C. vegetable broth
- 1 C. quinoa
- 1 C. shredded Cheddar cheese
- salt and ground black pepper to taste

Directions

- Boil the following in a large pot: quinoa, veggie broth, and broccoli.
- Once the broth is boiling set the heat to low and place a lid on the pot.
- Let the contents cook for 17 mins.
- Add in your cheese and put the lid back on.

- Let everything cook for 4 more mins then add pepper and salt.
- Enjoy.

Amount per serving (4 total)

Timing Information:

Preparation	Cooking	Total Time
5 m	20 m	25 m

Nutritional Information:

Calories	299 kcal
Fat	12.3 g
Carbohydrates	32.9g
Protein	14.8 g
Cholesterol	30 mg
Sodium	491 mg

* Percent Daily Values are based on a 2,000 calorie diet.

Broccoli-Cauliflower Salad (new)

Ingredients

1 C. broccoli florets

1 C. cauliflower florets

2 C. hard-cooked eggs, diced (optional)

1 C. shredded Cheddar cheese

6 slices bacon

1 C. mayonnaise

1/2 C. white sugar

2 tbsps white wine vinegar

Directions

Stir fry your bacon until fully done and crispy, break the bacon into pieces, and remove it from the pan.

Get a bowl, combine: bacon, broccoli, cheese, cauliflower, and eggs.

Get a 2nd bowl, combine: vinegar, mayo, and sugar. Stir the mix until it smooth then pour it over your broccoli mix.

Toss the contents then serve.

Enjoy.

Amount per serving (8 total)

Timing Information:

Preparation	Cooking	Total Time
10 m	15 m	25 m

Nutritional Information:

Calories	400 kcal
Fat	33 g
Carbohydrates	15.5g
Protein	11.2 g
Cholesterol	177 mg
Sodium	453 mg

* Percent Daily Values are based on a 2,000 calorie diet.

BROCCOLI CHEESE SOUP III

Ingredients

- 4 C. fresh broccoli, cut into bite size pieces
- 1 1/2 qt. chicken broth
- 2 C. milk
- 2 (10.75 oz.) cans condensed cream of celery soup
- 4 tbsps cornstarch
- 1/2 C. cold water
- 2 C. shredded Cheddar cheese

Directions

- Get a big pot and boil your broccoli in the broth for 12 mins.
- Now get a bowl, combine: celery soup and milk. Stir the contents until everything is smooth then mix some water and cornstarch together. Pour the mix in the

celery soup mix and stir everything.
- Let the contents continue to heat until everything is simmering then add your cheese. Once the cheese has melted shut the heat and stir everything.
- Enjoy.

Amount per serving (12 total)

Timing Information:

Preparation	Cooking	Total Time
10 m	30 m	40 m

Nutritional Information:

Calories	153 kcal
Fat	9.4 g
Carbohydrates	10.1g
Protein	7.5 g
Cholesterol	29 mg
Sodium	529 mg

* Percent Daily Values are based on a 2,000 calorie diet.

Sweet and Creamy Broccoli

Ingredients

- 1 (15 oz.) can creamed corn
- 2 eggs, beaten
- 2 tbsps white sugar
- 2 tbsps all-purpose flour
- 1 tsp salt
- 1/2 C. shredded mild Cheddar cheese
- 1/2 (10 oz.) package frozen chopped broccoli

Directions

- Set your oven to 350 degrees before doing anything else.
- Get a bowl, combine: salt, corn, flour, eggs, and sugar.
- Stir the mix then add in your broccoli and cheese.
- Stir the contents again then enter everything into a baking dish.

- Cook the mix for 65 mins.
- Enjoy.

Amount per serving (5 total)

Timing Information:

Preparation	Cooking	Total Time
10 m	1 h 10 m	1 h 20 m

Nutritional Information:

Calories	183 kcal
Fat	6.2 g
Carbohydrates	26.5g
Protein	8 g
Cholesterol	86 mg
Sodium	847 mg

* Percent Daily Values are based on a 2,000 calorie diet.

Broccoli in Venice

Ingredients

- 12 oz. rigatoni pasta
- 1/2 lb fresh broccoli florets
- 1/4 C. olive oil
- 1 tbsp minced garlic
- 2 tbsps pesto
- 1 C. chopped tomatoes
- 3/4 C. grated Parmesan cheese
- 1 lb boneless chicken breast halves, cooked and chopped
- salt to taste
- ground black pepper to taste

Directions

- Boil your pasta in water and salt for 9 mins then remove all the liquids.
- At the same time blanch your broccoli in the pasta water then

begin to stir fry your pesto sauce and garlic, in olive oil, for 4 mins.
- Now add in your tomatoes and cook everything for 30 more secs then place it all to the side.
- Get a bowl, combine: garlic mix, pasta, chicken, and broccoli.
- Stir the mix then add in the black pepper, salt, and parmesan.
- Stir everything again then serve.
- Enjoy.

Amount per serving (6 total)

Timing Information:

Preparation	Cooking	Total Time
10 m	30 m	40 m

Nutritional Information:

Calories	509 kcal
Fat	21.3 g
Carbohydrates	45.7g
Protein	34.4 g
Cholesterol	67 mg
Sodium	257 mg

* Percent Daily Values are based on a 2,000 calorie diet.

CREAM OF EVERYTHING CASSEROLE

Ingredients

- 2 C. water
- 2 C. uncooked instant rice
- 2 (10 oz.) cans chunk chicken, drained
- 1 (10.75 oz.) can condensed cream of mushroom soup
- 1 (10.75 oz.) can condensed cream of chicken soup
- 1/4 C. butter
- 1 C. milk
- 1 (16 oz.) package frozen chopped broccoli
- 1 small white onion, chopped
- 1 lb processed cheese food

Directions

- Set your oven to 350 degrees before doing anything else.

- Get your water boiling, then add in the rice, place a lid on the pot, and shut the heat.
- Let the rice sit for 10 mins.
- Now layer the following in a casserole dish: onions, rice, cheese, butter, cream of chicken, broccoli, chicken, milk, and mushroom soup.
- Cook the layers in the oven for 40 mins.
- Enjoy.

Amount per serving (8 total)

Timing Information:

Preparation	Cooking	Total Time
15 m	30 m	45 m

Nutritional Information:

Calories	756 kcal
Fat	30.8 g
Carbohydrates	82.7g
Protein	36 g
Cholesterol	110 mg
Sodium	1642 mg

* Percent Daily Values are based on a 2,000 calorie diet.

Seattle Style Broccoli Soup

Ingredients

- 3 (10 oz.) packages frozen chopped broccoli
- 3 (14.5 oz.) cans chicken broth
- 6 tbsps margarine
- 1 onion, chopped
- 1/2 C. all-purpose flour
- 2 C. milk
- 1 1/2 lbs processed cheese food (eg. Velveeta), cubed
- 1 pinch ground white pepper

Directions

- Get your broccoli boiling in broth, once the mix is boiling, set the heat to a lower level, and let the mix cook for 17 mins.
- Now being to stir fry your onions in butter for 7 mins then add the

flour to the onions and slowly add in the milk.
- Continue to heat and stir the mix until everything is thick.
- Now combine everything with the broccoli and add the cheese and pepper.
- Enjoy.

Amount per serving (8 total)

Timing Information:

Preparation	Cooking	Total Time
10 m	30 m	40 m

Nutritional Information:

Calories	475 kcal
Fat	24.4 g
Carbohydrates	33.8g
Protein	29.7 g
Cholesterol	54 mg
Sodium	2001 mg

* Percent Daily Values are based on a 2,000 calorie diet.

GREEN AND WHITE BROCCOLI

Ingredients

- 1/2 C. uncooked white rice
- 10 oz. broccoli florets
- 10 oz. cauliflower florets
- 1/2 C. butter
- 1 onion, chopped
- 1 lb processed cheese food, cubed
- 1 (10.75 oz.) can condensed cream of chicken soup
- 5 3/8 fluid oz. milk
- 1 1/2 C. crushed buttery round crackers

Directions

- Get your rice boiling in water, place a lid on the pot, set the heat to low, and let the rice cook for 22 mins.
- Then remove any extra liquids.

- Begin to boil your cauliflower and broccoli for 12 mins.
- Now set your oven to 350 degrees before doing anything else.
- Begin to stir fry your onions in butter then add the broccoli mix and the rice as well.
- Stir everything then add the rice and stir everything again.
- Add in the milk, cheese, and chicken soup. Then pour everything into a casserole dish and place the crackers over the mix.
- Cook the casserole in the oven for 35 mins.
- Enjoy.

Amount per serving (8 total)

Timing Information:

Preparation	Cooking	Total Time
40 m	30 m	1 h 10 m

Nutritional Information:

Calories	545 kcal
Fat	38.8 g
Carbohydrates	30g
Protein	20.5 g
Cholesterol	101 mg
Sodium	1544 mg

* Percent Daily Values are based on a 2,000 calorie diet.

Maggie's Easy Beef and Broccoli

Ingredients

- 1/3 C. oyster sauce
- 2 tsps Asian (toasted) sesame oil
- 1/3 C. sherry
- 1 tsp soy sauce
- 1 tsp white sugar
- 1 tsp cornstarch
- 3/4 lb beef round steak, cut into 1/8-inch thick strips
- 3 tbsps vegetable oil, plus more if needed
- 1 thin slice of fresh ginger root
- 1 clove garlic, peeled and smashed
- 1 lb broccoli, cut into florets

Directions

- Get a bowl, combine: cornstarch, oyster sauce, sugar, sesame oil, soy sauce, and sherry.
- Add the steak to the mix and place a covering on the bowl. Let the steak sit in the fridge for 40 mins.
- Now being to stir fry your garlic and ginger in veggie oil for 2 mins then throw them away.
- Add the broccoli to the oil and cook it for 8 mins.
- Now place the broccoli to the side and add some more oil.
- Begin to stir fry your meat for 6 mins.
- Then add the veggies back in and continue cooking the dish for 4 more mins.
- Enjoy.

Amount per serving (4 total)

Timing Information:

Preparation	Cooking	Total Time
15 m	15 m	1 h

Nutritional Information:

Calories	331 kcal
Fat	21.1 g
Carbohydrates	13.3g
Protein	21.7 g
Cholesterol	52 mg
Sodium	419 mg

* Percent Daily Values are based on a 2,000 calorie diet.

CREAMY BROCCOLI

Ingredients

- 1/2 C. butter
- 1 C. all-purpose flour
- 11 C. water
- 3 cubes chicken bouillon
- 2 lbs skinless, boneless chicken breast halves - cut into bite-size pieces
- 2 heads fresh broccoli, cut into florets
- 1 1/2 tsps salt
- 1 tsp ground black pepper
- 1 C. light cream
- 3 C. shredded Cheddar cheese

Directions

- Being to stir and heat your flour and butter in a large pot.
- Once the mix is thick place the contents to the side.

- Now add the following to the same pot: pepper, water, salt, bouillon, broccoli, and chicken.
- Get everything boiling, set the heat to low, and cook the mix for 50 mins.
- Slowly add in the flour mix and let the soup get thick.
- Continue to cook the contents for 7 mins, then lower the heat, and add the cream.
- Gradually add in the cheese one C. at a time then stir the mix until everything is melted.
- Enjoy.

Amount per serving (6 total)

Timing Information:

Preparation	Cooking	Total Time
10 m	1 h	1 h 10 m

Nutritional Information:

Calories	434 kcal
Fat	26.6 g
Carbohydrates	15.3g
Protein	33.4 g
Cholesterol	129 mg
Sodium	1059 mg

* Percent Daily Values are based on a 2,000 calorie diet.

American Casserole

Ingredients

- 4 heads fresh broccoli, chopped
- 1 1/2 C. shredded American cheese
- 1 (10.75 oz.) can condensed cream of mushroom soup
- 1 1/2 tsps salt
- 2 tsps ground black pepper
- 3 tbsps butter
- 2 C. crushed, seasoned croutons

Directions

- Set your oven to 350 degrees before doing anything else.
- Boil your broccoli in water and salt for 2 mins then remove all the liquids.
- In a large pot begin to heat the following: pepper, cheese, salt, and cream of mushroom.

- Heat and stir the mix until the cheese is completely melted.
- Now add the broccoli, stir the mix again, and pour everything into a casserole dish.
- Get another pot and melt your butter in it.
- Once the butter is melted add the croutons and get them evenly coated.
- Top the casserole with the buttered croutons and cook everything in the oven for 35 mins.
- Enjoy.

Amount per serving (12 total)

Timing Information:

Preparation	Cooking	Total Time
15 m	40 m	55 m

Nutritional Information:

Calories	202 kcal
Fat	12.6 g
Carbohydrates	15.7g
Protein	8.4 g
Cholesterol	28 mg
Sodium	973 mg

* Percent Daily Values are based on a 2,000 calorie diet.

CREAM OF MUSHROOMS AND BROCCOLI

Ingredients

- 1/2 (16 oz.) package linguine
- 1 C. fresh or frozen broccoli flowerets
- 2 tbsps butter
- 1 lb skinless, boneless chicken breast, cut into cubes
- 1 (10.75 oz.) can cream of mushroom soup
- 1/2 C. milk
- 1/2 C. grated Parmesan cheese
- 1/4 tsp ground black pepper

Directions

- Boil your pasta in water and salt for 5 mins then add in the broccoli and cook the mix for 5 more mins.
- Now remove all the liquids.

- Begin to stir fry your chicken in butter then once the meat is browned and done add: the pasta mix, cream of mushroom, black pepper, milk, and cheese.
- Add a topping of parmesan and serve.
- Enjoy.

Amount per serving (4 total)

Timing Information:

Preparation	Cooking	Total Time
	20 m	20 m

Nutritional Information:

Calories	645 kcal
Fat	42.7 g
Carbohydrates	39.7g
Protein	28.3 g
Cholesterol	151 mg
Sodium	355 mg

* Percent Daily Values are based on a 2,000 calorie diet.

Countryside Broccoli Soup

Ingredients

- 2 C. chopped onion
- 2 tbsps margarine
- 2 1/2 lbs peeled and cubed potatoes
- 5 C. boiling water
- 4 cubes chicken bouillon
- 3 C. fresh broccoli, cooked and drained
- salt and pepper to taste
- 3 C. shredded Cheddar cheese

Directions

- In a saucepan, begin to stir fry your onions in butter.
- Let the onions cook until they are see-through then add the bouillon, water, and potatoes.
- Break the bouillon apart and get everything boiling.

- Once the mix is boiling place a lid on the pot and set the heat to low.
- Let the mix cook for 17 mins.
- Now cut off the hard outer skin from broccoli stems and boil the broccoli in water for 6 mins. Then add it to the soup.
- Begin to puree the soup with an immersion blender then add the pepper and salt. You can also use a food processor and blend the soup in batches then place the pureed mix into a new pot.
- Combine in the cheese after the soup has been pureed and get everything hot again.
- Enjoy.

Amount per serving (4 total)

Timing Information:

Preparation	Cooking	Total Time
10 m	40 m	50 m

Nutritional Information:

Calories	448 kcal
Fat	22.8 g
Carbohydrates	42.6g
Protein	20.3 g
Cholesterol	60 mg
Sodium	1189 mg

* Percent Daily Values are based on a 2,000 calorie diet.

Southeast Asian Broccoli

Ingredients

- 12 oz. boneless, skinless chicken breast halves, cut into bite-sized pieces
- 1 tbsp oyster sauce
- 2 tbsps dark soy sauce
- 3 tbsps vegetable oil
- 2 cloves garlic, chopped
- 1 large onion, cut into rings
- 1/2 C. water
- 1 tsp ground black pepper
- 1 tsp white sugar
- 1/2 medium head bok choy, chopped
- 1 small head broccoli, chopped
- 1 tbsp cornstarch, mixed with equal parts water

Directions

- Get a bowl, combine: soy sauce, chicken, and oyster sauce.
- Let the mix stand for 20 mins.
- Now begin to stir fry your onions and garlic in oil until the onions are see-through.
- Turn up the heat and add in the chicken with its marinade.
- Cook the mix for 12 mins, until the chicken is fully done, then add the sugar, bok choy, broccoli, pepper, and water.
- Let the mix cook for 12 mins then add the cornstarch mix.
- Continue cooking everything for 7 mins.
- Enjoy.

Amount per serving (8 total)

Timing Information:

Preparation	Cooking	Total Time
10 m	25 m	35 m

Nutritional Information:

Calories	170 kcal
Fat	7.9 g
Carbohydrates	9.8g
Protein	16.2 g
Cholesterol	33 mg
Sodium	418 mg

* Percent Daily Values are based on a 2,000 calorie diet.

Alfredo Broccoli

Ingredients

- 1/2 lb dry fettuccine pasta
- 1 C. fresh chopped broccoli
- 2 tbsps butter
- 1 skinless, boneless chicken breasts
- 1 (10.75 oz.) can condensed cream of mushroom soup
- 1/2 C. milk
- 1/2 C. grated Parmesan cheese

Directions

- Boil your pasta in water and salt for 5 mins then add in the broccoli and continue boiling the mix for 5 more mins.
- Now remove all the liquids.
- Slice the chicken breast into cubes then begin to stir fry the meat in butter until it is fully done.

- Now add the cheese, milk, and soup.
- Stir the contents then add the pasta mix.
- Get everything hot then plate the dish.
- Enjoy.

Amount per serving (4 total)

Timing Information:

Preparation	Cooking	Total Time
10 m	20 m	30 m

Nutritional Information:

Calories	417 kcal
Fat	15.5 g
Carbohydrates	49.7g
Protein	21.1 g
Cholesterol	44 mg
Sodium	727 mg

* Percent Daily Values are based on a 2,000 calorie diet.

Artisan Style Broccoli Soup II

Ingredients

- 2 C. chicken broth
- 2 1/2 C. fresh broccoli
- 1/4 C. chopped onion
- 1 C. milk
- 2 tbsps all-purpose flour
- 1 C. shredded Cheddar cheese
- 1/2 tsp dried oregano
- salt and pepper to taste

Directions

- Get your broth boiling then add in the onions and broccoli.
- Let the mix boil for 6 mins.
- Now get a bowl, combine: flour and milk.
- Stir the mix until everything is smooth then add the mix to the broth.

- Stir everything then let the soup cook until it reaches your preferred level of thickness.
- Now add your cheese and let it melt.
- Finally add the spices (pepper, salt, oregano).
- Enjoy.

Amount per serving (4 total)

Timing Information:

Preparation	Cooking	Total Time
10 m	20 m	30 m

Nutritional Information:

Calories	161 kcal
Fat	9.2 g
Carbohydrates	9.1g
Protein	10.8 g
Cholesterol	28 mg
Sodium	481 mg

* Percent Daily Values are based on a 2,000 calorie diet.

Sour Cream Condensed Broccoli

Ingredients

- 2 (10 oz.) packages chopped frozen broccoli, thawed
- 1 (15.25 oz.) can whole kernel corn, drained
- 1 large onion, diced
- 1 (16 oz.) container sour cream
- 1 (10.75 oz.) can condensed cream of broccoli soup
- 2 C. shredded Cheddar cheese, divided
- 1 (6 oz.) package herb-seasoned dry bread stuffing mix
- 1/4 C. butter, melted

Directions

- Set your oven to 350 degrees before doing anything else.

- Get a bowl, combine: onions, broccoli, and corn.
- Stir the contents then add in 1/4 C. shredded cheese, soup, and sour cream.
- Get a 2nd bowl, combine: the melted butter and stuffing.
- Layer your broccoli into a baking dish then top the veggies with the stuffing.
- Cook everything in the oven for 35 mins then add the rest of the cheese and continue cooking the contents for 3 more mins until the cheese is melted.
- Enjoy.

Amount per serving (8 total)

Timing Information:

Preparation	Cooking	Total Time
15 m	35 m	50 m

Nutritional Information:

Calories	372 kcal
Fat	23.6 g
Carbohydrates	30.1g
Protein	12.4 g
Cholesterol	57 mg
Sodium	791 mg

* Percent Daily Values are based on a 2,000 calorie diet.

Asian Style Broccoli and Beef

Ingredients

- 1 tbsp olive oil
- 1 lb round steak, thinly sliced into 2 inch pieces
- salt to taste
- ground black pepper to taste
- 1 large onion, thinly sliced
- 2 C. fresh broccoli florets, chopped
- 1 (10.75 oz.) can condensed cream of broccoli soup
- 1/4 C. water
- 3 tbsps soy sauce

Directions

- Begin to stir fry your steak in olive oil then add in your pepper and salt.

- Let the meat fry until it is mostly done.
- Now add your onions and continue frying until they are soft.
- Then add in the soy sauce, broccoli, water, and broccoli soup.
- Stir the contents then place a lid on the pot.
- Let the mix cook until the broccoli is done.
- Enjoy.

Amount per serving (6 total)

Timing Information:

Preparation	Cooking	Total Time
15 m	20 m	45 m

Nutritional Information:

Calories	240 kcal
Fat	12.2 g
Carbohydrates	15.1g
Protein	17.4 g
Cholesterol	42 mg
Sodium	1179 mg

* Percent Daily Values are based on a 2,000 calorie diet.

Red Pepper Broccoli

Ingredients

- 1 (16 oz.) package frozen broccoli, thawed, cleaned, dried
- 1 tbsp olive oil
- 1/2 tsp crushed red pepper flakes
- salt, to taste

Directions

- Add your pepper flakes to your olive oil and let the mix cook for 60 secs then add in the broccoli and let it cook for 6 mins.
- After the broccoli has cooked add your salt then serve.
- Enjoy.

Amount per serving (6 total)

Timing Information:

Preparation	Cooking	Total Time
5 m	5 m	10 m

Nutritional Information:

Calories	61 kcal
Fat	3.8 g
Carbohydrates	5.6g
Protein	3.2 g
Cholesterol	0 mg
Sodium	27 mg

* Percent Daily Values are based on a 2,000 calorie diet.

Crackers and Broccoli Bake

Ingredients

- 2 (10 oz.) packages frozen chopped broccoli
- 8 oz. processed cheese food, shredded
- 1/4 lb butter
- 32 buttery round crackers, crushed

Directions

- Set your oven to 350 degrees before doing anything else.
- Layer your broccoli in a baking dish then top the veggies with the processed cheese.
- Now begin to stir fry your crushed crackers in butter, for 1 min, while stirring, then top the broccoli with the mix.

- Cook everything in the oven for 35 mins.
- Enjoy.

Amount per serving (8 total)

Timing Information:

Preparation	Cooking	Total Time
10 m	40 m	50 m

Nutritional Information:

Calories	330 kcal
Fat	25.6 g
Carbohydrates	16g
Protein	9.4 g
Cholesterol	56 mg
Sodium	577 mg

* Percent Daily Values are based on a 2,000 calorie diet.

BASIL BROCCOLI

Ingredients

- 8 tbsps olive oil
- 2 tbsps butter
- 4 cloves garlic, minced
- 1 lb fresh broccoli florets
- 1 C. vegetable broth
- 1 C. chopped fresh basil
- 1 lb rigatoni pasta
- 2 tbsps grated Parmesan cheese

Directions

- Boil your pasta in water and salt for 9 mins then remove all the liquids.
- Now heat and stir your butter and oil.
- Once the mix is hot begin to stir fry your broccoli and garlic for 4 mins then pour in the broth and get everything boiling.

- Once the mix is boiling, place a lid on the pot, set the heat to low, and let the contents cook until the broccoli is soft.
- Top the dish with the parmesan and serve.
- Enjoy.

Amount per serving (6 total)

Timing Information:

Preparation	Cooking	Total Time
10 m	20 m	30 m

Nutritional Information:

Calories	608 kcal
Fat	29.4 g
Carbohydrates	74.2g
Protein	16.1 g
Cholesterol	14 mg
Sodium	191 mg

* Percent Daily Values are based on a 2,000 calorie diet.

A Quiche of Broccoli

Ingredients

- 2 large potatoes, peeled
- 2 C. chopped fresh broccoli
- 1/4 C. milk
- 1/4 tsp salt
- 1 tbsp olive oil
- 1/2 onion, chopped
- 1 C. shredded Cheddar cheese
- 3 eggs
- 1 C. milk
- 1/2 tsp salt
- 1/2 tsp ground black pepper
- 1/4 tsp ground nutmeg

Directions

- Set your oven to 350 degrees before doing anything else.
- Boil your potatoes in water and salt for 17 mins then remove all the liquids.

- At the same time steam your broccoli, using a steamer insert, in a pot of 2 inches of boiling water.
- Steam the veggies for 5 mins then remove all the liquids.
- Begin to mash your potatoes and then add in some salt and continue mashing. Then combine in the milk and mash everything again.
- Coat a pie dish with olive oil then layer your potatoes at the bottom of the dish.
- Add some more olive oil then cook the crust in the oven for 32 mins.
- Then layer your cheese, onions, and broccoli in the pie dish.
- Get a bowl, combine: the nutmeg, eggs, pepper, milk, and salt.
- Pour this mix into the pie dish and cook everything in the oven for 35 mins.
- Let the quiche cool for 15 mins.
- Enjoy.

Amount per serving (4 total)

Timing Information:

Preparation	Cooking	Total Time
20 m	1 h 15 m	1 h 35 m

Nutritional Information:

Calories	320 kcal
Fat	14.7 g
Carbohydrates	33.5g
Protein	14.8 g
Cholesterol	140 mg
Sodium	575 mg

* Percent Daily Values are based on a 2,000 calorie diet.

Maggie's Easy Broccoli Stir Fry

Ingredients

- 1 lb broccoli florets
- 3 tbsps finely grated Parmesan cheese
- 1 tsp brown sugar
- 2 tbsps olive oil
- 1 tsp red pepper flakes
- 1/4 tsp kosher salt
- 1/8 tsp freshly ground black pepper

Directions

- Blanch your broccoli in boiling water for 60 seconds then immediately enter the veggies into some ice water.
- Now lay the broccoli on some paper towel to drain it completely.

- Get a bowl, combine: brown sugar and parmesan.
- Now get your oil hot then begin to stir fry the broccoli for a few secs then add in the black pepper, salt, and pepper flakes.
- Stir the broccoli then let everything cook for 3 mins.
- Shut the heat and top the veggie with the parmesan mix.
- Enjoy.

Amount per serving (4 total)

Timing Information:

Preparation	Cooking	Total Time
15 m	10 m	25 m

Nutritional Information:

Calories	81 kcal
Fat	5.6 g
Carbohydrates	6.2g
Protein	3.2 g
Cholesterol	2 mg
Sodium	< 144 mg

* Percent Daily Values are based on a 2,000 calorie diet.

2 Cheese Chicken Casserole

Ingredients

- 6 oz. egg noodles
- 3 tbsps butter
- 1 yellow onion, chopped
- 1/4 C. all-purpose flour
- 1 1/2 C. chicken broth
- 3/4 C. milk
- salt and pepper to taste
- 5 C. cooked, shredded chicken breast meat
- 1 (10 oz.) package chopped frozen broccoli, thawed
- 1 C. shredded Cheddar cheese
- 1 C. shredded provolone cheese

Directions

- Boil your pasta in water and salt for 9 mins. Then remove all the liquids.

- Coat a baking dish with oil then set your oven to 400 degrees before doing anything else.
- Now begin to stir fry your onions in butter for 4 mins then add in the flour.
- Stir the contents then pour in the broth.
- Stir the contents again until everything is smooth then begin to gradually add in your milk while continuing to stir.
- Once the mix becomes thick with a medium level of heat add some pepper and salt.
- Layer your pasta in your baking dish then place the chicken on top.
- Add the broccoli over the chicken and coat everything with the broth mix.
-
- Mix your cheese together then add 1/2 of the mix over the broccoli.

- Cook the layers in the oven for 25 mins then add the rest of the cheese and let the casserole stand for 10 mins inside the oven with no heat.
- Enjoy.

Amount per serving (8 total)

Timing Information:

Preparation	Cooking	Total Time
20 m	20 m	40 m

Nutritional Information:

Calories	580 kcal
Fat	28.6 g
Carbohydrates	30.1g
Protein	49.4 g
Cholesterol	164 mg
Sodium	453 mg

* Percent Daily Values are based on a 2,000 calorie diet.

Restaurant Style Broccoli

Ingredients

- 1 head fresh broccoli, cut into florets
- 1/4 C. butter, melted
- 2 tbsps lemon juice
- 1 tsp lemon zest
- 1/4 C. blanched slivered almonds

Directions

- With a steamer insert and large pot with 2 inches of boiling water.
- Steam the broccoli for 6 mins. Then remove all the liquids.
- Now melt your butter and add the almonds, lemon zest, and lemon juice. Combine all the contents and pour the mix over your broccoli.
- Enjoy.

Amount per serving (6 total)

Timing Information:

Preparation	Cooking	Total Time
5 m	10 m	15 m

Nutritional Information:

Calories	170 kcal
Fat	15.2 g
Carbohydrates	7g
Protein	3.7 g
Cholesterol	31 mg
Sodium	107 mg

* Percent Daily Values are based on a 2,000 calorie diet.

Parmesan Rabe

Ingredients

- 1 lb broccoli rabe, trimmed
- 5 tbsps extra virgin olive oil
- 1 clove garlic, minced
- 1 tbsp grated Parmesan cheese

Directions

- Slice two diagonal crisscross incisions into your broccoli rabe. Then cook the rabe in boiling salted water for 7 mins. Then remove all the liquids.
- Being to stir fry your garlic in olive oil for 3 mins then add the rabe and cook everything for 13 mins.
- Add your parmesan then serve.
- Enjoy.

Amount per serving (6 total)

Timing Information:

Preparation	Cooking	Total Time
20 m	20 m	40 m

Nutritional Information:

Calories	192 kcal
Fat	17.2 g
Carbohydrates	5.6g
Protein	4.5 g
Cholesterol	1 mg
Sodium	< 53 mg

* Percent Daily Values are based on a 2,000 calorie diet.

Swiss Style Broccoli Casserole

Ingredients

- 8 C. fresh broccoli
- 1/2 C. butter
- 2 tbsps all-purpose flour
- 1 small onion, chopped
- 1 1/4 C. milk
- salt and pepper to taste
- 4 C. shredded Swiss cheese
- 2 eggs, beaten

Directions

- Set your oven to 325 degrees before doing anything else.
- Steam your broccoli over 2 inches of boiling water, with a steamer insert, for 5 mins. Then remove all the liquids.
- Now being to stir and heat your flour and butter in a large pot.

Continue stirring and heating until the mix is bubbling then add the onions and milk.
- Get everything boiling and let it go for 60 secs.
- Now shut the heat and add in some pepper and salt.
- Combine in the eggs and cheese and add in the broccoli.
- Stir the mix again then place everything into a baking dish.
- Cook the broccoli for 40 mins in the oven.
- Enjoy.

Amount per serving (8 total)

Timing Information:

Preparation	Cooking	Total Time
15 m	30 m	45 m

Nutritional Information:

Calories	441 kcal
Fat	33 g
Carbohydrates	15g
Protein	23.3 g
Cholesterol	148 mg
Sodium	285 mg

* Percent Daily Values are based on a 2,000 calorie diet.

Thanks for Reading! Now Let's Try some Sushi and Dump Dinners....

Send the Book!

To grab this **box set** simply follow the link mentioned above, or tap the book cover.

This will take you to a page where you can simply enter your email address and a PDF version of the **box set** will be emailed to you.

I hope you are ready for some serious cooking!

[Send the Book!](#)

You will also receive updates about all my new books when they are free.

Also don't forget to like and subscribe on the social networks. I love meeting my readers. Links to all my profiles are below so please click and connect :)

[Facebook](#)

[Twitter](#)

Come On...
Let's Be Friends :)

I adore my readers and love connecting with them socially. Please follow the links below so we can connect on Facebook, Twitter, and Google+.

Facebook

Twitter

I also have a blog that I regularly update for my readers so check it out below.

My Blog

CAN I ASK A FAVOUR?

If you found this book interesting, or have otherwise found any benefit in it. Then may I ask that you post a review of it on Amazon? Nothing excites me more than new reviews, especially reviews which suggest new topics for writing. I do read all reviews and I always factor feedback into my newer works.

So if you are willing to take ten minutes to write what you sincerely thought about this book then please visit our Amazon page and post your opinions.

Again thank you!

INTERESTED IN OTHER EASY COOKBOOKS?

Everything is easy! Check out my Amazon Author page for more great cookbooks:

For a complete listing of all my books please see my author page.

Printed in Great Britain
by Amazon